FINDING SANCTUARY *in the Midst of Alzheimer's*

"Congregations are uniquely positioned to provide support for people with dementia and their spouses. Yet, many pastors and congregations feel inadequate in providing the spiritual and emotional support needed. Finding Sanctuary in the Midst of Alzheimer's is an excellent resource for individuals and congregations who want to be in ministry with this growing population. It is more than a how-to book; it is an avenue into the world of dementia where God's redemptive presence creates community and transforms both the caregivers and those receiving the care. I highly recommend this resource to every pastor and local congregation!"

—**Bishop (Retired) Kenneth L. Carder**,
author of *Ministry with the Forgotten:
Dementia through a Spiritual Lens*
(Abingdon Press, 2019)
Williams Distinguished Professor,
Emeritus, Duke Divinity School

"Elizabeth Shulman has written a compassionate and practical book to guide religious communities in supporting husbands, wives, and all family caregivers struggling to understand and cope with Alzheimer's disease. The number of family caregivers of someone with Alzheimer's disease is growing rapidly as the population ages. Most family caregivers are overwhelmed and need the support of their religious communities. Dr. Shulman describes a program of Bible study that can offer help to congregants by preparing leaders to reach out to caregivers. Caregiver stories set the stage for each section and promote deep insight and empathy. This book will help communities combat stigma and abandonment that is a common problem families face.

Finding Sanctuary is an outgrowth of the research she conducted when she was in seminary. Her stories of families illuminate the journey of husbands and wives as they adjust to changes in a loved one who is ill. As a nurse researcher on family caregiving, I found her book fascinating and very readable—her work resonated with my own research findings. The outcome of the program she describes will likely be a more supportive community and personal and spiritual growth for congregants. I highly recommend it."

— **Professor (Emeritus) Christine Williams**,
Christine E. Lynn College of Nursing,
Florida Atlantic University

"Finding Sanctuary in the Midst of Alzheimer's is a much-needed guide for family members caring for their companion or parent. In the confusion and anxiety related to Alzheimer's disease, there cannot be enough guidance for the caregiver. They suffer tremendously in their need to care for their loved one. Sanctuary in the Midst of Alzheimer's gives them the spiritual guidance needed. Caregivers, in times of stress, question many things, including their faith. This program helps caregivers get on track with their own spirituality while caring for their loved one. Excellent program; would recommend for any dementia caregiver."

— **Mary Finn**, Director of Administrative
Services, Alois Alzheimer Center

"This study guide is a gem! It is just what a lot of congregations are looking for to engage hard-to-engage folks, build relationships among members, deepen healing ministry, and educate the whole congregation. Dr. Shulman brings decades of research and practical experience to bear in this approachable, user-friendly toolkit.

It's a tough subject, one that most folks hope they never need to learn much about. The local congregation may be one of the few places in a lot of communities that is equipped to provide loving leadership in tackling the nuts-and-bolts information, busting the myths, and moving participants from fear and shame to compassion and action.

On one level, this study guide is simply a practical approach to helping congregation members cope with a difficult family situation—but there's more to it than that. At a time when disorders impacting mental capacity are still stigmatized, this study guide can help congregations reconnect with their role as "sanctuaries"—safe spaces for those who are *suffering. And on a* deeper level, developing a ministry grounded in Shulman's process will allow people of faith to bridge the gap between its internal, member-focused ministries and the needs of the wider community.

As someone who works with communities of all faiths on developing justice ministries, I am constantly struck by how congregations miss the opportunity to connect their internal programming to their prophetic activities. Finding Sanctuary in the Midst of Alzheimer's is a perfect example of how providing comfort to specific individuals can build the congregation's ministry to a hurting world."

— **Bee Moorhead**, Executive Director
Texas Impact and Texas Interfaith Center for Public Policy

FINDING SANCTUARY

in the Midst of Alzheimer's

A Spiritual Guide
for Families
Facing Dementia

Elizabeth Shulman, D.Min., STNA

NASHVILLE

NEW YORK • LONDON • MELBOURNE • VANCOUVER

FINDING SANCTUARY
in the Midst of Alzheimer's

A Spiritual Guide for Families Facing Dementia

Published in New York, New York, by Morgan James Publishing. Morgan James is a trademark of Morgan James, LLC. www.MorganJamesPublishing.com

Morgan James BOGO™

A **FREE** ebook edition is available for you or a friend with the purchase of this print book.

CLEARLY SIGN YOUR NAME ABOVE

Instructions to claim your free ebook edition:
1. Visit MorganJamesBOGO.com
2. Sign your name CLEARLY in the space above
3. Complete the form and submit a photo of this entire page
4. You or your friend can download the ebook to your preferred device

ISBN 978-1-63195-463-4 paperback
ISBN 978-1-63195-464-1 eBook
Library of Congress Control Number:
2020924406

Cover Design by:
Rachel Lopez
www.r2cdesign.com

Morgan James PUBLISHING

Builds with... **Habitat for Humanity®** Peninsula and Greater Williamsburg

Morgan James is a proud partner of Habitat for Humanity Peninsula and Greater Williamsburg. Partners in building since 2006.

Get involved today! Visit
MorganJamesPublishing.com/giving-back

"Seek the peace and prosperity of the city to which I have carried you into exile. Pray to the Lord for it, because if it prospers, you too will prosper." (Jeremiah 29:7)

sanc·tu·ary
noun \ˈsaŋ(k)-chə-ˌwer-ē\
: a place where someone or something is protected or given shelter
: the protection that is provided by a safe place
: the room inside a church, synagogue, etc., where religious services are held (Merriam-Webster)

CONTENTS

PREFACE

Family members provide most of the care for persons with Alzheimer's disease and other forms of dementia. As symptoms such as forgetfulness, confusion, and personality changes take place, caregivers are left to grieve for a loved one who is physically present yet relationally disappearing. Research has shown that adult children caring for parents often report a deep sense of loneliness and increased conflict with other family members.[1]

---

1   A. S. Hwang, L. Rosenberg, P. Kontos, J. I. Cameron, A. Mihailidis, and L. Nygård, "Sustaining Care for a Parent with Dementia: An Indefinite and Intertwined Process," *International Journal of Qualitative Studies on Health and Well-Being* 12, sup. 2 (2017): 1389578; doi:1 0.1080/17482631.2017.1389578. Published correction appears in *International Journal of Qualitative Studies on Health and Well-Being* 12, no. 1 (2017): 1411003.

Many spousal caregivers of Alzheimer's patients struggle to make sense of their marriage as the disease progresses.[2]

During times of confusion and anxiety, many caregivers turn to their religious faith or spirituality as a means of coping.[3] However, most places of worship are not well equipped to address the impact of dementia on families. Current literature shares that caregivers often feel isolated from others; this includes feeling isolated from their church.[4] A person is diagnosed with Alzheimer's disease every 65 seconds.[5] With communities supporting an increasing number of aging citizens, it only makes sense that our places of worship would become centers of support for persons with dementia and their family members.

One evening before going to bed I posted this question on a Facebook dementia caregiving page: "What would you want your church to know about your experience as a dementia caregiver?" When I woke up the next morning, there were 260

2   Sheila LoboPrabhu, Victor Molinari, Kimberly Arlinghaus, and Ellen Barr, "Spouses of Patients with Dementia," *Journal of Gerontological Social Work* 44, no. 3/4 (2005): 162.

3   A. M. Banks, "Dementia and Religion: Inside a Church's Alzheimer's Caregiver Support Group," *Religion News*, January 17. 2019; https://religionnews.com/2019/01/17/dementia-and-religion-inside-a-churchs-alzheimers-caregiver-support-group.

4   K. Fogg Berry, *When Words Fail: Practical Ministry to People with Dementia and Their Caregivers* (Richmond, VA: Westminster Canterbury Foundation, 2018).

5   Alzheimer's Facts and Figures Report, The Alzheimer's Association, 2019.

responses, and some were entire paragraphs. In sharing their needs, most responders yearned for their church to provide better support. *Finding Sanctuary in the Midst of Alzheimer's* is a ministry that helps to fill this void for caregivers who are searching for spiritual support. It also equips congregations with the tools and direction they need to provide better support to caregivers in their communities.

This curriculum is a Bible study rooted in Scripture and framed by the personal experiences of caregivers. The Personal Narratives within this study were gathered from my doctoral research, my work as a hospice chaplain, and interactions with others on various dementia caregiver support groups on Facebook.

This program is meant to offer hope and prompt meaningful discussion. While I have used the Bible as the spiritual context, I hope that people of all backgrounds will benefit from this ministry and from the assurance that there is a higher power overseeing, loving, and providing a sense of meaning, regardless of your faith background.

Ultimately, I pray that these pages bring you encouragement, strength, and newfound meaning for your journey.

INTRODUCTION

Finding Sanctuary in the Midst of Alzheimer's is a five-week program. The entire curriculum is twofold in its ministry objectives. One purpose of the curriculum is to educate and train pastors and church members to more effectively and compassionately minister to those in their congregation who are caring for a family member with dementia. The other purpose is to create a safe place for family members to gather and share their experiences in a spiritually based environment. Because each section is self-contained, this book can be separated and tailored for individual groups such as senior centers, assisted living facilities, or support groups that would like to integrate a spiritual component. Additionally, I have phrased most of the questions to prompt self-reflection, so that if you are unable to be in a group, you can use this as a personal Bible study. (Note: Some of the scripture and narratives have been repeated for more than one group.) Ultimately, the goal of this ministry, when executed in its entirety, is to create a program that results in churches becoming an important resource for the growing number of dementia caregivers in their community.

Three Parallel Studies

This complete program is composed of three separate groups that each meet for four weeks. Each lesson is designed so that anyone can facilitate it. The only requirements to lead are making sure there are large sheets of paper, markers, and a willingness to read out loud if there are no volunteers. Allow one to one and a half hours for each lesson. After the four weeks, the three separate groups come together for a fifth week to discuss the results from each individual group and begin to create a plan of ministry. The three groups are:

1. **Providing Sanctuary:** For pastors, church members, or individuals who want to better understand the exprcience of caregiving and learn how to better support dementia caregivers.

2. **Seeking Sanctuary: Caring for a Parent:** For adult children or other family members facing such challenges

as: role reversal, loneliness and isolation, self-care and asking for help.

3. **Seeking Sanctuary: Support for Spouses:** For spouses encountering the unique challenges of caring for a husband or wife with dementia. This section explores the commitment of marriage while offering encouragement to spouses.

Bringing It All Together

In the fifth week, Creating Sanctuary, participants from the Providing and Seeking groups meet together. Using the information that each group has compiled during their separate gatherings, the combined group of providers and seekers discusses the challenges and needs currently present in their church and explores how the gifts that have been identified can be used to meet these needs. Because each group will be presenting information unique to their participants, the ministry created out of this gathering will be unique to that congregation. In other words, one church's dementia ministry may look very different from that of another church, despite completing the same program.

PART I

PROVIDING SANCTUARY
A Curriculum for Congregations

Lesson 1

HONOR THY MOTHER AND FATHER

Summary: This initial lesson explores your assumptions and impressions of what it is like for an adult child caring for a parent with Alzheimer's or another form of dementia. The first gathering is designed to guide participants to better appreciate caregiving challenges through reading aloud and discussing the personal accounts of caregivers.

Goals

- Assess the current level of participants' knowledge of dementia caregiving.
- Begin to create a list of challenges encountered by caregivers of Alzheimer's patients.

Materials
- Large sheets of paper
- Marker
- Nametags (if needed)

Lesson

A. Introductions

1. Go around the room and introduce yourselves by sharing your first name and who you know caring for someone with Alzheimer's or another form of dementia.

2. On a large sheet of paper, write the heading "Challenges." Take turns sharing what you perceive to be challenges for family members caring for a loved one with dementia. (Save this list and have it available for future lessons.)

B. Have a volunteer read 1 Corinthians 13:1–13:

If I speak in the tongues of men or of angels, but do not have love, I am only a resounding gong or a clanging cymbal. If I have the gift of prophecy and can fathom all mysteries and all knowledge, and if I have a faith that can move mountains, but do not have love, I am nothing. If I give all I possess to the poor and give over my body to hardship that I may boast, but do not have love, I gain nothing. Love is patient, love is kind.

It does not envy, it does not boast, it is not proud. It does not dishonor others, it is not self-seeking, it is not easily angered, it keeps no record of wrongs. Love does not delight in evil but rejoices with the truth. It always protects, always trusts, always hopes, always perseveres. Love never fails. But where there are prophecies, they will cease; where there are tongues, they will be stilled; where there is knowledge, it will pass away. For we know in part and we prophesy in part, but when completeness comes, what is in part disappears. When I was a child, I talked like a child, I thought like a child, I reasoned like a child. When I became a man, I put the ways of childhood behind me. For now we see only a reflection as in a mirror; then we shall see face to face. Now I know in part; then I shall know fully, even as I am fully known. And now these three remain: faith, hope and love. But the greatest of these is love.

C. Discuss:
   1. Name the descriptions of love given in this passage.
   2. Of the descriptions listed, which one(s) do you struggle with at times?
   3. Which verse brings you the greatest hope and why?
D. Take turns reading aloud the Personal Narratives in the next section.

1. After each narrative consider this question: "What stands out to you about this narrative?"
2. Return to the list of Challenges and write down any additional challenges that may have been identified while discussing the Narratives.

E. Read aloud Isaiah 58:10:

And if you spend yourselves in behalf of the hungry and satisfy the needs of the oppressed, then your light will rise in the darkness.

F. Discuss:

1. Who in your life best exemplifies a servant? How so?
2. Describe a time when your light rose in the darkness because of your service to someone.
3. How can we begin to better serve those in our community affected by Alzheimer's disease? (We will explore this more extensively in future lessons.)

G. Recite together in prayer: *Lord, thank you for the opportunity to learn more about our brothers and sisters who are facing the challenges of providing care for someone with dementia. Direct our time together toward a greater understanding of their experience, and show us how we can, both collectively and individually, be a light in the darkness for these caregivers. Amen.*

Lesson 1

Personal Narratives

After each narrative, ask yourself, "What stands out to me about this narrative?"

1.

My mom is the person I went to with all my problems. Now that she has dementia, I miss that about her. I miss so many things, actually. She taught me how to sew on buttons, showed me how to cook, babysat my kids. Now, I do all of these things for her. Don't get me wrong, I'm glad to do it, but I miss having my mom as I knew her for so many years.

2.

To be honest, Dad and I have not had the best relationship. He wasn't one to express his feelings and left it to Mom to handle most of the work of raising me and my sister. However, he *was* the one to dole out the punishment, and he firmly believed in the "spare the rod, spoil the child" philosophy—sometimes to the extreme, in my opinion. My sister moved hundreds of miles away right after high school. Mom died four years ago, and I've been the one who stayed close to home, so now Dad is my responsibility. I really don't like it, but what else can I do?

3.

I took Mom to the doctor's office, and he had all the facts together on X-rays and psych tests and all, and he looked at Mom and said, "Mrs. B, we think you're in the early stages of Alzheimer's disease." And Mom didn't panic or anything. She just said, "Well, I want everyone to know about it. I don't want the people at church saying, 'What's wrong with her?'" So, I just took my cue from her and told people. I've always believed in open communication. We get into trouble when we try to fake things and cover up and all that. It's best just to let it out. So, the people at church then learned to adapt to Mom.

4.

It's gotten too difficult to take Dad places, even places where everyone knows him. He'll either wander around or, if I try to keep him with me or sitting in one spot, he'll get combative and tell me to leave him alone. It's embarrassing when I'm out in public. People who don't understand my situation will just watch. They don't know what to say or how to help—even with his old buddies. I tried to take him to the diner where he used to gather with the guys. They greeted him and everything, but he didn't seem to remember them, although he can be good at covering it up; laughing and making very generic statements like, "Is that so?" Even still, they knew something was off, and you could tell they were a little uncomfortable, which then made me uncomfortable.

Lesson 2

'TIL DEATH DO US PART

Summary: This second week, we turn our attention from the experiences of children caring for a parent to spouses caring for a husband or wife and the unique challenges that spouses encounter. Married participants will spend time considering how their own marriage would be affected if they or their spouse were diagnosed with Alzheimer's.

Goals

- Identify qualities of a relationship unique to marriage.
- Explore how Alzheimer's can affect these qualities.
- Name expectations you have about your own future.

- Hypothesize the ways Alzheimer's might affect those expectations.
- Study and reflect on Jesus' description of marriage.
- Continue to identify challenges of caregivers.

Materials

- List of challenges from previous week
- Large sheets of paper
- Marker

Lesson

A. Go around the group and share: Which sitcom on TV (past or present) portrays your favorite image of marriage? Why?

B. Read aloud Matthew 22:23–33:

That same day the Sadducees, who say there is no resurrection, came to him with a question. "Teacher," they said, "Moses told us that if a man dies without having children, his brother must marry the widow and raise up offspring for him. Now there were seven brothers among us. The first one married and died, and since he had no children, he left his wife to his brother. The same thing happened to the second and third brother, right on down to the seventh. Finally, the woman died. Now then, at the resurrection, whose wife will she be of the seven, since all of them were married to her?" Jesus replied, "You are in error because you do not know the Scriptures or the power of God. At the resurrection people will neither marry nor be given in marriage; they will be like the angels in heaven. But about the resurrection of the dead—have you not read what God said to you, 'I am the God of Abraham, the God of Isaac, and the God of Jacob'? He is not the God of the dead but of the living." When the crowds heard this, they were astonished at his teaching.

C. Discuss:

  1. Why do you think there is no marriage in heaven?

  2. What makes marriage a marriage for you?

  3. How do you anticipate your senior years to be? If married, what plans or hopes do you and your spouse have in the future?

D. Consider this statistic: According to the Alzheimer's Association, the likelihood of developing late-onset Alzheimer's approximately doubles every five years after age 65. By age 85, the risk of developing Alzheimer's is nearly 50 percent. Consider:

  1. In what ways might a diagnosis of Alzheimer's for you or your spouse challenge and/or enhance your marriage?

  2. How might it change your plans for the future?

E. Take turns reading aloud the Personal Narratives in the following section.

   1. For each narrative, consider and discuss: "What stands out to you about this narrative?"

   2. Display the list of challenges from last week and add to the list if needed.

F. Read aloud James 1:26–27:

   Those who consider themselves religious and yet do not keep a tight rein on their tongues deceive themselves, and their religion is worthless. Religion that God our Father accepts as pure and faultless is this: to look after orphans and widows in their distress and to keep oneself from being polluted by the world.

   1. Discuss: In what ways have family caregivers become "widows" and "orphans"?

   2. On a large sheet of paper, write *Needs* at the top. Referring to the list of challenges, make a list of needs that correspond to the challenges listed. (Save these lists for future lessons.)

G. Recite together in prayer: *God, may we come to a greater understanding of what it is like to care for a loved one who may not remember who we are. Help us to remember and care for others without judgment and with an abundance of compassion. Amen.*

Lesson 2

Personal Narratives

After each narrative, ask yourself, "What stands out to me about this narrative?"

1.

My wife and I had great friends at church. We were inseparable. The church called us a clique. But it was a support thing, and they liked my wife and she was sharp. From time to time she'd come forth with something that would surprise us all. Otherwise, she was rather quiet. When I put her in the assisted living facility, the group didn't call me anymore. We'd eat sometimes Sunday after church if they were willing. These friends were ministers, one a retired chaplain and the other a missionary. I was talking to my daughter one night (she and her husband divorced many years ago), and when I mentioned to her the reaction I was getting from my friends she said, "That's just like being divorced." Now, I make rare contacts with those couples, but you know, there's no support there. My relationship with the church staff and with a lot of the church members... they don't seem to know what to say.

2.

Selfishly, I kind of wish God would just go ahead and take me. Seventy-four years in this world is long enough. But then who would take care of Mary? Those are the thoughts that keep me awake at night.

3.

I've become a mother to my husband instead of a wife. I find it's difficult to make this role change at this point in my life. In the attempt, I feel I'm not my usual self. I seem to have other thoughts that are taking over. They are sad and depressing, and I don't like the feeling. I feel very sorry for myself because I can't be what my husband needs me to be. I don't have the commitment, as you would have, for example, for a sick child. I don't have the strength anymore. I don't have the strength anymore to be a "mother" in that way, and certainly not to my husband.

4.

To me, sacrifice is the essence of marital love. It's not the essence, but it's part of it: doing what pleases the beloved. It's not just in sex; it's in everything. You do what pleases the beloved. If something bugs you, then I need to change. I need to, if for love's sake, change the way I do things- for you. You know we start out life—all of life is a loss, isn't it? We lose our hair, we lose our teeth, we lose our appearance, we lose our job, we lose a loved one. All of all of life is a losing process. But in Christ there is always a purpose even in the losing. Faith in Christ trumps all of that because we know that this is... we are temporary, and we are all terminal. We're going to die of something...Jesus was the consummate [sufferer]. All the people in the Scriptures who were usable by God were sufferers. He allowed them to be put through the hoops; including his own son. He suffered more than any of us. If Jesus suffered, I can glorify him by suffering, too.

Lesson 3

GIFTS TO GIVE

Summary: This week you have the opportunity to identify additional challenges and needs of caregivers. You are then invited to take the Spiritual Gifts Inventory (no small task!) to explore ways you might minister to these caregivers in your congregation.

Goals

- Identify additional challenges and needs of caregivers.
- Equip participants to respond compassionately and effectively to family caregivers through Scripture and the Spiritual Gifts Inventory.

Materials

- The challenges and needs list from the previous weeks (display during the lesson)
- Large sheets of paper
- Marker

Lesson

A. Display the lists of challenges and needs that you compiled during the previous weeks. Take turns reading the Personal Narratives and discuss what stands out to you in each narrative. Identify any new challenges and needs, and add them to the corresponding lists.

B. Read aloud 1 Corinthians 12:1–11:

Now about the gifts of the Spirit, brothers and sisters, I do not want you to be uninformed. You know that when you were pagans, somehow or other you were influenced and led astray to mute idols. Therefore, I want you to know that no one who is speaking by the Spirit of God says, "Jesus be cursed," and no one can say, "Jesus is Lord," except by the Holy Spirit. There are different kinds of gifts, but the same Spirit distributes them. There are different kinds of service, but the same Lord. There are different kinds of working, but in all of them and in everyone it is the same God at work. Now to each one the manifestation of the Spirit is given for the common good. To one there is given through the Spirit a message of wisdom, to another a message of knowledge by means of the same Spirit, to another faith by the same Spirit, to another gifts of healing by that one Spirit, to another miraculous powers, to another prophecy, to another distinguishing between spirits, to another speaking in different kinds of tongues, and to still another the interpretation of tongues. All these are the work of one and the same Spirit, and God distributes them to each one, just as God determines.

C. Discuss:

1. Which of the gifts that Paul mentions stand out to you and why? What are some of your gifts? (Note: God is infinite, and so provides infinite gifts. Paul may not have included your particular gift(s) in this short paragraph!)

2. What is the most fulfilling job you have ever had? What made it so? In what ways can you apply those qualities of fulfillment to serving others?

D. Review the instructions for the Spiritual Gifts Inventory at the end of this lesson. If there is extra time, begin taking it. Otherwise, plan to complete it at home and bring the results back next week. If you would rather take the Spiritual Gifts Inventory online, it is available on several websites. To find these, go to www.elizabethshulman.com.

E. Note that sometimes we may have gifts we do not realize we have. There are many spiritual gifts tests available online. While the Spiritual Gifts Inventory is lengthy, it is also comprehensive. After taking the test and tallying the results, you might question some of the results. It may be interesting to ask other group members next week if your results correspond with how they see you. (You may have some undiscovered gifts!) Next week, come with your results and prepared to brainstorm unique "gift-giving" opportunities that you (and your church) will be able to provide for dementia caregivers both within your congregation, as well as in the greater community.

F. Recite together in prayer: *God, give us perseverance and a sense of openness as we explore the unique gifts you have given to each one of us gathered here. May we discover new things about ourselves, and, more importantly, may we be inspired to share our gifts with others. Amen.*

Lesson 3

Personal Narratives

After each narrative, ask yourself, "What stands out to me about this narrative?"

1.

It was getting difficult to take her to church, especially since I was on staff there. Wednesday nights were a little more difficult because there weren't as many people to look after her during choir practice. For a few nights, she sat in on the rehearsals. My daughter started coming over on Wednesday nights and stayed with her, giving up her own choir, which she sang in during that period of time. My wife would go with me on Sundays. Some of the ladies in the Sunday school class would come and get her and take her to Sunday school and then sit with her in church. That worked out fine until we got into the fall and she started deteriorating and becoming more difficult to handle at church. Nobody would say that her behavior bothered them, but she would get a lot of looks. And to be honest, it was disruptive. But I didn't want to keep her from church!

2.

I just pray, "God, hold my hand." It gave me strength to keep going. The church encourages me by saying they're praying for me and this type of thing. That makes me feel internally better. But I still feel pretty alone and exhausted.

3.

Sometimes I just want someone to ask me how I am doing; not like when you bump into someone on the street and you chitchat and then go on. I know everyone is busy, and I'm not going to ask for their help anyway; I guess it's a pride thing. But it helps when people make me feel like they care about me. It's probably my ego, but it lifts me up.

4.

The church has just been the backbone. Our church is a real "people church." We have an Alzheimer's support group, we have a day center, and it's great. When I first started into all of this, they sent me a booklet on grief. And I'll get three more during the year. It's a series, which is so helpful. I would say that our church has just been fantastic.

Spiritual Gifts Inventory

Developed by Michael Anne Haywood with assistance from Genie Carr, Steve Gambino, Rev. Virginia Herring, Margaret Moore, Marjorie Northup, Mary at Stillpoint, and Jean Woods. Used with permission from Michael Anne Haywood.

1. There are 115 statements below. Circle the number for each question that best fits your response. On the Profile Sheet, Part 1 (p. 48), transfer your answers to the corresponding question.

2. Add across to total your scores for each of the gifts. Each gift will have a score between 0 and 20.

3. Order the gifts in descending order of score, one on each line (p. 49). Higher scores indicate your more dominant gifts.

This is an exhaustive list, and some of the questions may seem repetitive. Don't put too much thought into each question. Answer honestly and try not to answer how you think you *should* answer.

Spiritual Gifts Inventory	Strongly Agree	Agree Somewhat	Undecided	Disagree Somewhat	Strongly Disagree
1. I find great joy in leading people to accomplish group goals.	4	3	2	1	0
2. I feel called to be a leader in the church.	4	3	2	1	0
3. I look for opportunities to assist people who have trouble doing for themselves.	4	3	2	1	0

Spiritual Gifts Inventory	Strongly Agree	Agree Somewhat	Undecided	Disagree Somewhat	Strongly Disagree
4. I find that the repair and maintenance of things in my environment come easily to me.	4	3	2	1	0
5. It seems easy to perceive whether what a person is doing is honest or dishonest.	4	3	2	1	0
6. I enjoy sharing about God with people who are not churchgoers.	4	3	2	1	0
7. I enjoy motivating people to a higher spiritual commitment.	4	3	2	1	0
8. I try to do God's will, even when it's not the popular thing to do.	4	3	2	1	0

	Spiritual Gifts Inventory	Strongly Agree	Agree Somewhat	Undecided	Disagree Somewhat	Strongly Disagree
9.	It is very satisfying to me to give generously of my money for God's work.	4	3	2	1	0
10.	I enjoy the opportunity to pray with and for a person who is physically ill.	4	3	2	1	0
11.	I like having people in my home.	4	3	2	1	0
12.	I seem to recognize prayer needs instinctively.	4	3	2	1	0
13.	I enjoy learning new things of all kinds.	4	3	2	1	0
14.	I feel great compassion for the problems of others.	4	3	2	1	0
15.	I adapt easily in a culture different from mine.	4	3	2	1	0

Spiritual Gifts Inventory	Strongly Agree	Agree Somewhat	Undecided	Disagree Somewhat	Strongly Disagree
16. I like to sing hymns and songs either alone or with other people.	4	3	2	1	0
17. I enjoy having the responsibility of leading other people in their spiritual life.	4	3	2	1	0
18. I am ready to try the impossible, because I have great trust in God.	4	3	2	1	0
19. I like to talk about spirituality with other Christians.	4	3	2	1	0
20. I enjoy doing "chores" around the church.	4	3	2	1	0

Spiritual Gifts Inventory

		Strongly Agree	Agree Somewhat	Undecided	Disagree Somewhat	Strongly Disagree
21.	I'm excited in helping people to discover important insights in the Scriptures.	4	3	2	1	0
22.	I communicate easily with people of a different culture or language background.	4	3	2	1	0
23.	People with spiritual problems have come to me for advice and counsel.	4	3	2	1	0
24.	People seem to enjoy following my leadership in undertaking an important task.	4	3	2	1	0
25.	I feel that God gives me wisdom in leading people in spiritual matters.	4	3	2	1	0

Spiritual Gifts Inventory

		Strongly Agree	Agree Somewhat	Undecided	Disagree Somewhat	Strongly Disagree
26.	I enjoy helping with the emergency tasks around the church.	4	3	2	1	0
27.	I have enjoyed creating various kinds of arts and/or crafts.	4	3	2	1	0
28.	I seem to have a sense of the direction in which God is leading.	4	3	2	1	0
29.	I seem able to sense when the Spirit is leading a person to realize the holy in their lives.	4	3	2	1	0
30.	I have a knack for bringing out the best in others.	4	3	2	1	0
31.	I'm willing to keep trying, even when a task is tedious and seems unending.	4	3	2	1	0

Spiritual Gifts Inventory	Strongly Agree	Agree Somewhat	Undecided	Disagree Somewhat	Strongly Disagree
32. I share my possessions with others willingly.	4	3	2	1	0
33. I have prayed with a person who was in distress, and the person was comforted.	4	3	2	1	0
34. I do not feel uncomfortable when people drop in unexpectedly.	4	3	2	1	0
35. I pray for others often and for significant periods of time.	4	3	2	1	0
36. Through study I have learned many helpful insights.	4	3	2	1	0
37. Visiting people in retirement homes or the hospital gives me great satisfaction.	4	3	2	1	0

Spiritual Gifts Inventory	Strongly Agree	Agree Somewhat	Undecided	Disagree Somewhat	Strongly Disagree
38. It is easy for me to move into a new community and make friends.	4	3	2	1	0
39. God has given me the ability to play a musical instrument, and I enjoy it.	4	3	2	1	0
40. It is exciting to provide spiritual leadership for a congregation.	4	3	2	1	0
41. I am often ready to believe God will lead us through a situation that others feel is impossible.	4	3	2	1	0
42. I like to share Scripture to comfort or to encourage others.	4	3	2	1	0
43. I enjoy doing routine tasks for the glory of God.	4	3	2	1	0

Spiritual Gifts Inventory

	Strongly Agree	Agree Somewhat	Undecided	Disagree Somewhat	Strongly Disagree
44. I have enjoyed teaching individuals and/or classes.	4	3	2	1	0
45. I derive spiritual meaning from music, art, or nature.	4	3	2	1	0
46. I enjoy helping another to find solutions to difficult problems in life.	4	3	2	1	0
47. I like to organize people for more effective ministry.	4	3	2	1	0
48. I have little fear in leading people in spiritual matters.	4	3	2	1	0
49. I don't mind helping people who are sick or disabled.	4	3	2	1	0
50. I like to create things with my hands.	4	3	2	1	0
51. I seem to have a knack for sensing the difference between truth and error.	4	3	2	1	0

Spiritual Gifts Inventory	Strongly Agree	Agree Somewhat	Undecided	Disagree Somewhat	Strongly Disagree
52. I am drawn to share my faith in God with others.	4	3	2	1	0
53. I like to encourage inactive church members to become involved again.	4	3	2	1	0
54. I am sure of God's loving presence, even when things go wrong.	4	3	2	1	0
55. I appreciate the opportunity to give of my skills and energy in a critical situation.	4	3	2	1	0
56. I feel called to be a part of the healing ministry of the church.	4	3	2	1	0
57. People seem to feel very comfortable in my home.	4	3	2	1	0
58. God consistently answers my prayers in tangible ways.	4	3	2	1	0

Spiritual Gifts Inventory

		Strongly Agree	Agree Somewhat	Undecided	Disagree Somewhat	Strongly Disagree
59.	I have learned much about God from Scripture, books, and observing life.	4	3	2	1	0
60.	I sense joy in comforting people in difficult situations.	4	3	2	1	0
61.	I am able to relate to and communicate with people of different locations or cultures.	4	3	2	1	0
62.	I have enjoyed being involved with church, school, and/or local musical productions.	4	3	2	1	0
63.	I like to assist people with their spiritual problems.	4	3	2	1	0
64.	I believe that when I am doing God's will, God can and does work through me.	4	3	2	1	0

Spiritual Gifts Inventory	Strongly Agree	Agree Somewhat	Undecided	Disagree Somewhat	Strongly Disagree
65. I enjoy relating God's Word to the issues of the day and sharing this with others.	4	3	2	1	0
66. When there is something to be done for the church, I'm glad to help, but I don't want to be in charge.	4	3	2	1	0
67. It seems that people learn readily when I teach them.	4	3	2	1	0
68. I can communicate well with people who are limited by a physical or mental handicap.	4	3	2	1	0
69. I seem to be able to help people find the truths they seek.	4	3	2	1	0
70. I like the challenge of making important decisions.	4	3	2	1	0

Spiritual Gifts Inventory	Strongly Agree	Agree Somewhat	Undecided	Disagree Somewhat	Strongly Disagree
71. I appreciate the opportunity to share God's Word with others.	4	3	2	1	0
72. One of my ministries is helping other people to bear their burdens.	4	3	2	1	0
73. I like to spend time and money improving and beautifying things in God's creation.	4	3	2	1	0
74. I have helped people to discover God's will in their lives.	4	3	2	1	0
75. I have sometimes shared spiritual experiences with a neighbor who doesn't attend church.	4	3	2	1	0

Spiritual Gifts Inventory

	Strongly Agree	Agree Somewhat	Undecided	Disagree Somewhat	Strongly Disagree
76. People who are feeling perplexed often come to me for encouragement and comfort.	4	3	2	1	0
77. When everyone is discouraged—even me—I still trust God.	4	3	2	1	0
78. If I cannot give much money to support God's work, I give generously of my time.	4	3	2	1	0
79. I feel peace when I am with a person who is sick or injured.	4	3	2	1	0

Spiritual Gifts Inventory	Strongly Agree	Agree Somewhat	Undecided	Disagree Somewhat	Strongly Disagree
80. When missionaries or church leaders come to our church I like (or would like) to have them come to my home.	4	3	2	1	0
81. I faithfully pray for others recognizing that their effectiveness and total well-being depends on God.	4	3	2	1	0
82. Knowledge of the Bible and of church teachings helps me to solve problems in daily life and in the life of the church.	4	3	2	1	0
83. People seem to think I am a kind, compassionate person.	4	3	2	1	0

Spiritual Gifts Inventory	Strongly Agree	Agree Somewhat	Undecided	Disagree Somewhat	Strongly Disagree
84. The thought of beginning a new church in a new community is exciting to me.	4	3	2	1	0
85. I feel secure that my musical ability will be of benefit to other people with whom I come in contact.	4	3	2	1	0
86. People like to bring their troubles and concerns to me because they feel I care.	4	3	2	1	0
87. People seem to think of me as one who believes that with God everything is possible.	4	3	2	1	0
88. It is important for me to speak out against wrong when I see it in the world.	4	3	2	1	0

Spiritual Gifts Inventory

	Strongly Agree	Agree Somewhat	Undecided	Disagree Somewhat	Strongly Disagree
89. I find more satisfaction in doing a job myself than in finding someone else to do it.	4	3	2	1	0
90. One of the joys of my ministry is training people to be more effective in living out their faith.	4	3	2	1	0
91. I can make sense of specialized information (like computers, blueprints, accounting, etc.).	4	3	2	1	0
92. I feel that I have insight in selecting workable alternatives in difficult situations.	4	3	2	1	0

Spiritual Gifts Inventory	Strongly Agree	Agree Somewhat	Undecided	Disagree Somewhat	Strongly Disagree
93. When I am in a disorganized group, I tend to be the first one to step forward to get us organized.	4	3	2	1	0
94. I enjoy training workers in the congregation.	4	3	2	1	0
95. If a family is facing a serious crisis, I enjoy the opportunity to help them.	4	3	2	1	0
96. I find pleasure in designing, creating, or decorating things.	4	3	2	1	0
97. I often look beneath the surface and discover richer meanings.	4	3	2	1	0

Spiritual Gifts Inventory	Strongly Agree	Agree Somewhat	Undecided	Disagree Somewhat	Strongly Disagree
98. I feel a deep concern for the people in my community who have not been attracted by the church.	4	3	2	1	0
99. I am sort of like a cheerleader, cheering others on when they are doing something well.	4	3	2	1	0
100. Even when it seems that my prayer isn't answered, I keep praying.	4	3	2	1	0
101. I give sacrificially of my time, talents, and resources, because I know that God will meet my needs.	4	3	2	1	0
102. I feel strongly that my prayers for a sick person are important.	4	3	2	1	0

Spiritual Gifts Inventory

		Strongly Agree	Agree Somewhat	Undecided	Disagree Somewhat	Strongly Disagree
103.	I have opened my home to someone in need.	4	3	2	1	0
104.	I find myself praying even while I am doing other things.	4	3	2	1	0
105.	I find it an enjoyable challenge to read and study a difficult book of the Bible.	4	3	2	1	0
106.	I find great satisfaction in visiting people who are confined to their homes.	4	3	2	1	0
107.	I have a strong desire to meet people of other communities and countries and to talk about our respective understandings of God.	4	3	2	1	0

Spiritual Gifts Inventory

	Strongly Agree	Agree Somewhat	Undecided	Disagree Somewhat	Strongly Disagree
108. I have a knack for selecting appropriate and inspiring music for worship services or for parish events.	4	3	2	1	0
109. I enjoy a close relationship with people in a one-on-one situation.	4	3	2	1	0
110. I will take on a difficult task for the church, because God will give me the ability to see it through.	4	3	2	1	0
111. I feel called to stand up for what is right, even if it irritates others.	4	3	2	1	0
112. I like to do things without attracting much attention.	4	3	2	1	0

Spiritual Gifts Inventory	Strongly Agree	Agree Somewhat	Undecided	Disagree Somewhat	Strongly Disagree
113. It is easy to organize materials for teaching a Bible class.	4	3	2	1	0
114. I have a knack for foreign languages—or ASL or Braille.	4	3	2	1	0
115. I have confidence in dealing with problems.	4	3	2	1	0

Spiritual Gifts Profile Sheet
Part 1

The numbers on this sheet correspond to the numbers of the statements in the inventory. Put your scores for each question into the following table, then compute the sum of each row. This provides your score for each spiritual gift.

1__	24__	47__	70__	93__	=	__	Administration
2__	25__	48__	71__	94__	=	__	Apostle
3__	26__	49__	72__	95__	=	__	Caregiver
4__	27__	50__	73__	96__	=	__	Craftsmanship
5__	28__	51__	74__	97__	=	__	Discernment
6__	29__	52__	75__	98__	=	__	Evangelist
7__	30__	53__	76__	99__	=	__	Exhortation
8__	31__	54__	77__	100__	=	__	Faith
9__	32__	55__	78__	101__	=	__	Giving
10__	33__	56__	79__	102__	=	__	Healing
11__	34__	57__	80__	103__	=	__	Hospitality
12__	35__	58__	81__	104__	=	__	Intercession
13__	36__	59__	82__	105__	=	__	Knowledge
14__	37__	60__	83__	106__	=	__	Mercy
15__	38__	61__	84__	107__	=	__	Missionary
16__	39__	62__	85__	108__	=	__	Musician
17__	40__	63__	86__	109__	=	__	Pastor
18__	41__	64__	87__	110__	=	__	(Deeds of) Power
19__	42__	65__	88__	111__	=	__	Prophet
20__	43__	66__	89__	112__	=	__	Serving
21__	44__	67__	90__	113__	=	__	Teacher
22__	45__	68__	91__	114__	=	__	Tongues
23__	46__	69__	92__	115__	=	__	Wisdom

Spiritual Gifts Profile
Part 2

In the spaces below, list the five highest-scoring gifts from the highest score to the lowest.

Score	Gift

Interpreting the Numbers

16–20: You are doing this, or you might enjoy trying it.

11–15: This may come easily to you.

6–10: You may have to work hard to do this gracefully.

0–5: You probably would not enjoy doing this.

Lesson 4

WAYS TO SERVE

Summary: This week is committed to creative "gift giving." Your group will discuss the gifts that each of you identified from the Spiritual Gifts Inventory and then look at ways to apply these gifts to the needs of dementia caregivers in your community.

Goals

- Identify the gifts of each group member.
- Encourage creativity in matching spiritual gifts with caregiver needs.
- Empower each other to use your gifts to serve dementia caregivers.

Materials

- Spiritual Gifts Inventory results
- Large sheets of paper
- Marker

Lesson

A. Read aloud James 2:14–17:

What good is it, my brothers and sisters, if someone claims to have faith but has no deeds? Can such faith save them? Suppose a brother or a sister is without clothes and daily food. If one of you says to them, "Go in peace; keep warm and well fed," but does nothing about their physical needs, what good is it? In the same way, faith by itself, if it is not accompanied by action, is dead.

B. Discuss:

1. Name a time someone came to your need. How did it leave you feeling?

2. Toward what type of person or group of people do you feel the most compassion?

3. When have you been challenged to put your faith into action? Why was it a challenge?

C. Review the results of each participant's Spiritual Gifts Inventory. If the group has more than six members, break into groups of three or four, and then return to the original group to discuss the following:

1. Share the top 5 gifts revealed to you from the Inventory. Were there any surprises in your results?

2. Is there anyone who is confused by their results or wonders what their gifts mean? If so, ask fellow participants for input.

3. Write "Gifts to Give" on a large sheet of paper. Make a list of the gifts represented by the group.

D. Ministry Exploration

1. Display the challenges and needs lists from previous weeks next to the gifts to give list. Place a fourth large sheet of paper next to the other three and write "Ways to Serve" at the top of the sheet.

2. Referring to the challenges, needs, and gifts to give lists, write down where your gifts meet the needs of caregivers on the fourth sheet. Expand your discussion to also consider the gifts that you think your congregation as a whole has to offer.

3. It is often difficult for caregivers (or anyone!) to ask for help. Spend time reflecting on your own level of comfort in asking for help, and explore ways to reach out effectively to those who may decline help out of a sense of pride or embarrassment or for another reason.

4. Be prepared to bring these four lists to week 5, Creating Sanctuary, if your church is completing the entire *Finding Sanctuary in the Midst of Alzheimer's* program.

E. Recite together in prayer: *Lord, thank you for the gifts you have given uniquely to me. May I embrace these gifts and find new ways to share them, knowing that in sharing my gifts, I am experiencing your love more fully. Remind us all that we truly are your hands and your feet and that when we serve others, we serve you. Amen.*

PART II

SEEKING SANCTUARY
Caring for a Parent

Lesson 1

ROLE REVERSAL

Summary: When an adult is diagnosed with dementia, it can be a very slow process of parents becoming more dependent on their children for care. Having been used to being cared *for*, children (or other younger relatives) may find it very difficult to take care of the adults they have always looked to as authority figures. This can be particularly hard when those caregiving duties include things such as restricting activities, feeding, and bathing. This lesson explores this change of roles and how adult children can feel more comfortable in their caregiving activities.

Goals

- Become acquainted with other group members.
- Assess your level of comfort in your current caregiving situation.
- Explore challenges of caring for a parent.

Materials

- Large sheets of paper
- Marker
- Nametags (if needed)

Lesson

A. Go around the room and answer the following questions: For whom do you provide care? If you had unlimited finances, what caregiving duty would you pay someone else to do?

B. Read aloud Narrative 1 (in the next section) and discuss the following:

1. What stands out to you in this narrative?

2. How would you describe your current level of responsibility for caregiving? Checking in occasionally? Providing 24-hour care? Something in between?

3. What has been the most difficult adjustment for you as a caregiver?

C. Read Narratives 2 and 3. After each one, consider:

   1. What stands out to you in this narrative?

   2. In what ways can you relate to these narratives?

D. Read Deuteronomy 5:16:

   Honor your father and your mother, as the Lord your God has commanded you, so that you may live long and that it may go well with you in the land the Lord your God is giving you.

E. Read Ephesians 6:1–3:

   Children, obey your parents in the Lord, for this is right. "Honor your father and mother"—which is the first commandment with a promise—"so that it may go well with you and that you may enjoy long life on the earth."

F. Discuss:

   1. The Ephesians version points out that the commandment to "honor your father and mother" is "the first commandment with a promise." What is that promise, and why do you think this unique addendum was added to this particular commandment?

   2. What traits or advice did you receive from your parents that you are using as a caregiver now with them?

3. What is unique about you that makes you a very capable caregiver for your parent?

G. Read Narrative 4 and discuss:

1. How do you relate or not relate to this person's perspective on caregiving for their parent?

2. Consider Psalm 139:16, which says, "…all the days ordained for me were written in your book before one of them came to be." How would you feel if you believed the thought, "Caregiving for my parent is precisely what should be happening in my life right now"?

H. Read Narrative 5 and discuss the following:

1. What stands out to you in this narrative?

2. In what ways could you practice honoring your mother or father by allowing them to lead the way?

I. On a large sheet of paper, write "I wish others knew _____ about my caregiving experience." Write down the answers from the group. (Save this list for week 5.)

J. Recite together in prayer: *Lord, thank you for this time to meet together with others who are in a similar situation. May we find comfort and strength through listening to one another's experiences and through the promise that you are always with us. Amen.*

Lesson 1
Personal Narratives

After each narrative, ask yourself, "What stands out to me about this narrative?"

1.

I can remember my mom blowing on my daughter's food before she fed her. Yesterday, I found myself doing that for my mother! Little things like that, such as brushing her hair, holding her hands to steady her as she walks, answering her endless questions, even telling her she can't do something because it's not safe…all these things she did for me when I was a child, and now I do them for her. I'm glad I can do it for her, but it still feels a little uncomfortable at times.

2.

Yesterday was the hardest day ever. I took the car keys away from my dad. It had to be done; he kept driving places and getting lost or coming home with a new scratch on the car. One time a few months ago, a police officer pulled him over for driving 25 miles per hour on the freeway. What's so frustrating is that my dad just does not get it! He thinks he is fine to drive and is furious with me. How can I make him understand? He says he's not talking to me until I give him back his keys. I took the car to my house, thinking, "Out of sight, out of mind." No such luck, yet. I feel horrible.

3.

I am a part of the "sandwich generation." Not only am I worrying about what my youngest is up to in college, or how my other son is coping as a brand new father, but I'm also scared that my father (who was just diagnosed with early-stage Alzheimer's) will forget how to get home when he goes on his daily walk or if he'll remember to turn off the stove. I don't know how *not* to worry.

4.

This is not the way it was supposed to be.

5.

My mother hasn't known who I am for almost a year. It was heartbreaking at first. Then she started thinking I was her sister, and I'd explain over and over that I was her daughter (plus, her sister had died years ago!). Trying to get her to believe something that her brain no longer knew made it worse. Once I stopped trying to convince her who I was, she seemed to enjoy me more. And having her enjoy our visits became more important to me than her knowing how I was related to her. That has been the biggest lesson for me—it's not how *she* sees the situation (she has dementia—she can't help it!); rather, it's *how I respond* that determines how our interactions go. Now, when I visit with her, I let her lead the way and I just go with it. In a weird way, it feels like I'm honoring her more by doing that instead of constantly arguing with her about what is reality. We both enjoy the visits more.

Lesson 2

LONELINESS AND ISOLATION

Summary: Feeling separated from others is one of the most common experiences for caregivers. This can lead to an acute sense of loneliness and feelings of isolation. This lesson encourages you to identify areas where you feel most isolated and explore ways to reduce loneliness.

Goals

- Identify areas where you feel most lonely.
- Explore ways to lessen feelings of loneliness and isolation.

Materials

- Large sheets of paper
- Markers

Lesson

A. Consider: How would you describe yourself? Social butterfly? Loner? Something in between? How comfortable are you asking others for help?

B. Read Genesis 2:18:

The Lord God said, "It is not good for man to be alone. I will make a helper suitable for him."

C. Read Psalm 68:5–6:

A father to the fatherless, a defender of widows, is God in his holy dwelling. God sets the lonely in families, he leads out the prisoners with singing.

D. Discuss:

1. When do you feel most alone?

2. Right now, as a caregiver, on a scale of 1–10, with 1 being completely alone and 10 being not at all lonely, where do you fall?

3. According to the passage in Genesis, God did not intend for humans to be alone. With whom do you enjoy the greatest companionship? Why this person? In the Psalm, God "leads out the prisoners with singing." In what ways does God lead you

out of challenging situations? What activity or occasion makes your heart sing?

E. Read aloud the Personal Narratives for this lesson in the following section and discuss. After each narrative, discuss: "What stands out to you about this narrative?"

F. On the top of two large sheets of paper, write the following sentences, one on each sheet: "What are my caregiving strengths?" and "How can my community make me an even better caregiver?" List the answers that are given. (Save these lists for week 5.)

G. Recite together in prayer: *Lord, you have told us that "wherever two or three are gathered you are among them." Thank you for our community together today. Just as Jesus went off alone to pray before ministering to others, help us to use our times alone to draw nearer to you and find strength, so that we may minister to others in a way that gives us hope and satisfaction in our caregiving responsibilities. Amen.*

Lesson 2

Personal Narratives

After each narrative, ask yourself, "What stands out to me about this narrative?"

1.

Unless you've lived it, it's inexplicable. You love them unconditionally but they are absent; sometimes present as who they were, but mostly gone. It's lonely and isolating. Heartbreaking. People judge you for your decisions if you are not a constant martyr. Gosh, the things I would love. A break. A meal. A visit. A freaking call from an old friend. It amazes me how many friends of my 68-year-old father are nonexistent.

2.

I've been taking care of Mom for going on two years. My sister used to come over and help, but lately she feels that since Mom is "still around," she should go to a nursing home if I'm getting tired, because "this could go on for years." My sister seems to have this attitude of "Well, you're the one who wanted to care for Mom, so go for it."

3.

I wish others would ask about us, too. Everyone asks how Mom is doing, which is great, of course. The handful of times (in eight years) that someone has asked me how I'm doing has resulted in a flash-outburst of tears—because no one ever asks about me. Of course, I get that "this" isn't about me, but the toughest part about being strong (because only the strong step up to this challenge) is that everyone thinks we're invincible. Well, we *are*—on the outside. Inside is another story. We're lonely and isolated. We need love and TLC, too.

4.

After feeling resentful about people not coming to visit, I realized that if you aren't a caregiver for someone with dementia—or heck, if you are never even around someone with dementia—then you just don't get it. But I don't know how to make people understand. I truly believe that if people understood, they would want to help.

Lesson 3

ASKING FOR HELP

Summary: Most people have trouble asking for help. The reasons caregivers don't ask for help are varied. This lesson considers why caregivers may be hesitant to ask help and explores ways to help you find the courage to reach out to others.

Goals
- Identify reasons why it is difficult to ask for help.
- List ways others can help you.

Materials
- Large sheets of paper
- Markers

Lesson

A. On the top of a large sheet of paper, write "Why caregivers don't ask for help." On the top of another sheet, write "Something that would help me a lot is_____."

B. Take turns reading aloud each Narrative. For each narrative, discuss:

   1. What stands out to you about this narrative?

   2. What reason is being given for why the person is reluctant to ask for help? Record the answers on the first large sheet. (Add reasons why *you* don't ask for help, if it has not been listed.)

   3. What random act of kindness would mean the most to you? Record the answers on the second sheet, as well as other ways someone could provide help to a caregiver.

C. Read Psalm 107:28–30:

   Then they cried to the Lord in their trouble, and he brought them out of their distress. He stilled the storm to a whisper; the waves of the sea were hushed. Then they were glad when it grew calm, and he guided them to their desired haven.

D. Discuss:

   1. How often do you reach out to God in distress?

   2. What time of day is most quiet for you?

3. Take a moment to practice quietness. Have someone keep time. Close your eyes. Imagine a place that makes you feel peaceful. Remain there and breathe slowly for two minutes. Then open your eyes.

4. How did those two minutes feel for you? Describe your perfect "haven?" How possible is it for you to find two minutes to be still and breathe slowly during your day?

E. Read Galatians 6:2:

Carry each other's burdens, and in this way, you will fulfill the law of Christ.

F. Discuss:

1. What responsibilities do you have as a caregiver to make your needs known?

2. In what way is asking for God's help different from asking a human for their help?

3. In what way is it the same?

4. To whom do you feel the most comfortable asking for help? Why this person?

G. Recite together in prayer: *Lord, sometimes I feel so alone. I know in my heart you are always with me, but sometimes I have a hard time feeling it. Remind me to trust you and to be still and know that you are God. In moments when I feel overwhelmed, encourage me to stop, close my eyes, and breathe so that you can reveal yourself to me. Please show me opportunities to reach out when I need help, give me the courage to do so, and connect me with those seeking to serve. Amen.*

Lesson 3
Personal Narratives

After each narrative, ask yourself, "What stands out to me about this narrative?"

1.

Last week my dad made a huge mess while going to the bathroom. He was a police officer for 28 years and was a very stoic, proper kind of man. Dementia has robbed him of so many of the qualities that made him who he is. I was embarrassed for him, because he would be mortified if he knew I had to clean up after him. My sister, who lives out of town, tells me I should hire a caregiver, but not only is it expensive; everyone in our small town *knows* Dad. Well, at least, knows the old Dad.

2.

I've asked for help, and it makes me feel so bad for even having to ask. A few times the person I asked for help didn't follow through or gave me an excuse for not being able to help. And it took me so long to actually reach out! It's like being rejected for a date after summoning up the courage to ask. After a while, it honestly just seems easier to do it myself.

3.

My husband and I have been caring for my mother for four years. We know her and her quirks better than anyone else. It's a catch-22; we are exhausted doing care 24/7, but no one else can do it as well. I love my sister dearly, but the one time she stayed with my mom so my husband and I could go out of town for a family reunion, it took over a week to get Mom back to her routine, eating and sleeping normally and not acting weird.

4.

There is no earthly way I would be able to have someone come and sit with my dad. His dementia has made him so suspicious and when his confusion is at its worst, he can be combative. There HAS to be a way for me to get help, I just haven't found it yet.

Lesson 4

SELF–CARE

Summary: Often, caregivers put everyone else first—at the expense of their own well-being. Yet, Jesus set a strong example of self-care (See Matt. 14:23, Mark 1:35, and Luke 5:16). We are created in God's image, and it is our responsibility to recognize that no one else can be *you*. When you take care of yourself first, you will be better able to serve others.

Goals
- Appreciate your uniqueness
- Recognize the importance of self-care
- Identify specific activities that feed your soul.

Materials
- Large sheets of paper
- Markers
- Notebook-sized sheet of paper for each participant
- Pens

Lesson

A. Read Mark 12:30–31:

"Love the Lord your God with all your heart and with all your soul and with all your mind and with all your strength." The second is this: "Love your neighbor as yourself." There is no commandment greater than these.

B. Distribute one sheet of paper and a pen to each participant.

1. Position your papers horizontally and draw two lines from the top of the page to the bottom, separating the paper into three columns. At the top of the left column write, "Ways I love the Lord with all my heart, soul, and strength." At the top of the middle column write "Ways I love myself." And at the top of the right column, write "Ways I love my neighbor."

2. Take five to seven minutes to write your responses and then take turns sharing your responses with the group.

3. Discuss: Which column was the easiest to fill in and which was the most difficult? Why?

4. Think of a "neighbor" (friend, acquaintance, etc.) for whom you would do anything. Would you do the same for yourself? Why or why not?

5. Consider and then describe what taking the best care of yourself for three hours would look like.

6. What would you need to do in order to experience those three hours? How can your "neighbors" help you?

C. Take turns reading aloud this week's Personal Narratives. After each one, discuss:

1. What stands out to you about this narrative?

2. What action did the caregiver have to take to ensure self-care?

D. On a large sheet of paper, write "Common Challenges for Caregivers." Based on the Narratives and personal experiences shared these past weeks write down specific challenges that you and others encounter as a caregiver. (Bring this list along with the lists from previous lessons to week 5.)

E. Consider these quotes from Norman Vincent Peale and Wayne Dyer, respectively: "Change your thoughts, and you change your world" and "Change the way you look at things, and the things you look at change."

   1. On a large sheet of paper, draw a line down the center of the paper. In the left column, write a list of thoughts you may have during the times of frustration, worry, fear, etc.; for example, "This feels like it's never going to end."

   2. After completing that list, in the right column change each negative thought into one that is positive or expresses hope. For example, "This feels like it's never going to end" can become "This too shall pass" or "One day at a time."

   3. Consider which statements feel better. Practice observing your thoughts this coming week and see if you can tweak them into ways that are more positive.

F. On another large sheet of paper, make a list of activities that feed your spirits; for example, taking a walk, watching sports, or seeing grandchildren. Explore with each other how you might sneak some of these activities into your week.

G. Recite together in prayer: *Lord, I know you did not bring me into this world to feel hopeless. Help me to see my caregiving situation through your eyes. Give me your vision and lead me to experiences that will show me how I cannot only survive but thrive in my role as a caregiver. Amen.*

Lesson 4
Personal Narratives

After each narrative, ask yourself, "What stands out to me about this narrative?"

1.

I grew up in a proud family with a strong work ethic. Self-sacrifice was something to be admired. It may not be surprising that my dad died of a heart attack in his 50s. But after some heart issues myself, I got to the point where I was not going to sacrifice my own health for my mom. I love her dearly, but I could no longer let the person with dementia control this situation. She had become combative when I tried to dress or bathe her, and I was constantly worrying about her wandering outside. I never thought I would do it, but I finally placed her in a nursing facility. The biggest surprise? She adapted (fairly) well and our visits are pleasant and enjoyable. I'm not sure she knows exactly who I am. I will say, this is not the case for my older sister. Mom cries every she visits for some reason. Now, I still have some worries—different worries—that come from her not living with me, but overall, I have found that being able to have time for myself gives me the opportunity to have better, more quality time with her.

2.

I am a loss what to do. My mom was diagnosed with vascular dementia a few years ago. She has some confusion, but is still able to care for herself, for the most part. This spring, we sold Mom's house and she moved in with me and my husband. Now that my mom is with us, she gets very jealous when I go to my weekly luncheon with my girlfriends. She doesn't understand why she can't come with me and tries to lay a guilt trip on me each time I go. Last week she said to me, "Try to have a good time while your husband babysits me." Ugh! I leave anyway!

3.

The other day, I found myself sitting on a camping chair at Costco eating a sample from one of the food counters. It was a rare occurrence when my brother had agreed to stay with our dad for a couple of hours so I could run some errands. Hilariously, I slid down in the chair, looked up at the ceiling and the thought, "This is the life!" I guess the more difficult life gets, the easier it is to find joy in little things. My husband jokes that lowering our standards is the key to happiness!

4.

I often dream of running off and escaping my current life; hiring a 24-hour caregiver for my dad and taking a cruise. The cost of a caregiver alone makes it too expensive for me to even consider. And then yesterday, my neighbor brought over some cookies while my dad and I were sitting outside. She said to me, "Why don't you go take a 30-minute stroll while your father and I sit here and watch the birds?" I surprised myself and took her up on the offer. It made a world of difference. It may not have been a cruise, but that 30-minute "vacation" was wonderful.

PART III

SEEKING SANCTUARY
Support for Spouses

Lesson 1

GOD WITH US

Summary: This first week is an introductory lesson on the overall experience of having a spouse with Alzheimer's or another form of dementia. Marriage is a unique, intimate relationship, and others may not understand your challenges. The Personal Narratives in this chapter present a variety of struggles to initiate conversation.

Goals

- Become acquainted with other group members.
- Establish this gathering as a safe place where you can each share your thoughts and stories in a confidential setting.

- Identify experiences common to spouses in their role as caregivers.
- Affirm God's presence

Materials
- Large sheets of paper
- Marker

Lesson

A. Establish a verbal agreement of confidentiality within the group.

B. Go around the room and share:
   1. Your first name
   2. The number of years you have been married
   3. The number of years since your partner was diagnosed with Alzheimer's/dementia

C. Take turns reading aloud the Personal Narratives below.
   1. For each narrative, consider what stands out to you in that particular narrative, and share how you relate or do not relate to it.
   2. On the large sheet of paper, write "Common Experiences." Underneath, make a list of common experiences spouses encounter based on the narratives. Feel free to add your own. (Save this list for future meetings.)

D. Read aloud Luke 24:13–32:

Now that same day two of them were going to a village called Emmaus, about seven miles from Jerusalem. They were talking with each other about everything that had happened. As they talked and discussed these things with each other, Jesus himself came up and walked along with them; but they were kept from recognizing him. He asked them, "What are you discussing together as you walk along?" They stood still; their faces downcast. One of them, named Cleopas, asked him, "Are you the only one visiting Jerusalem who does not know the things that have happened there in these days?" "What things?" he asked. "About Jesus of Nazareth," they replied. "He was a prophet, powerful in word and deed before God and all the people. The chief priests and our rulers handed him over to be sentenced to death, and they crucified him; but we had hoped that he was the one who was going to redeem Israel. And what is more, it is the third day since all this took place. In addition, some of our women amazed us. They went to the tomb early this morning but didn't find his body. They came and told us that they had seen a vision of angels, who said he was alive. Then some of our companions went to the tomb and found it just as the women had said, but they did not see

Jesus." He said to them, "How foolish you are, and how slow to believe all that the prophets have spoken! Did not the Messiah have to suffer these things and then enter his glory?" And beginning with Moses and all the Prophets, he explained to them what was said in all the Scriptures concerning himself. As they approached the village to which they were going, Jesus continued on as if he were going farther. But they urged him strongly, "Stay with us, for it is nearly evening; the day is almost over." So, he went in to stay with them. When he was at the table with them, he took bread, gave thanks, broke it and began to give it to them. Then their eyes were opened and they recognized him, and he disappeared from their sight. They asked each other, "Were not our hearts burning within us while he talked with us on the road and opened the Scriptures to us?"

E. Discuss:

1. Why do you think the disciples don't recognize Jesus immediately?

2. Where is God in your life right now? Are you desperately seeking him? Is he easily visible? You wouldn't mind a surprise appearance?

3. When you have trouble recognizing God's presence, is it for similar reasons as the disciples'? How or how not?

4. Complete the sentence: "For where two or three gather in my name, _____" (Matt. 18:20).

5. How can this group help you recognize God's presence more fully?

F. Refer back to Narrative 5. Encourage participants to experiment with keeping a journal.

G. Recite together in prayer: *Lord, thank you for this time together. The challenge of caring for my spouse sometimes draws my attention away from you. Help me to remember that you are present in every moment of my day and to know that my struggles are there to bring me closer to you. Thank you for each person gathered here. May we find comfort and strength in each other's stories. Amen.*

Lesson 1
Personal Narratives

After each narrative, ask yourself, "What stands out to me about this narrative?"

1.

Marriage to me is companionship. I realize now that I took for granted the comfort of just sitting with Margaret watching TV in the evenings. I miss the routine. After years of marriage, you get used to things being a certain way. I don't like change.

2.

I guess religion and stuff really helped me. I mean, I just knew God was helping. My religion helped me cope, although

I couldn't leave Alice at home to go to church. I didn't have anybody helping me. I just felt like God was watching over me. And every time I came up against something, and I just didn't think I was going to make it, it would just seem like somebody would just take over and things would get better. I'd go on and things would be okay. But I often worry about what will happen if it gets to be too much for me. Because it's exhausting. I don't think anybody realizes how lonely and exhausting it all is.

3.

My husband has become someone I don't even recognize. He has always been so stoic and quiet. But recently his behavior has changed as his dementia has gotten worse. He has started to lash out when I try to help him get dressed. He even tried to swing at me once! It has to be horrible to lose your mind. And I feel sad for him. But I also get angry because I'm just trying to help him!

4.

I think my wife, Helen, hid her dementia for a long time. One day my daughter mentioned, "You know, Mom doesn't really answer questions. She just laughs when I ask her something." After that, I started seeing that Helen was vague about a lot of things. When we were in groups, she would look to me to respond. It happened so gradually that I now wonder if I missed things I should have seen sooner.

5.

I kept a journal from day one. I went home that night and went to Walmart and bought a journal. The first entry is July 12, 1995 (the date of my wife's diagnosis). And every day, every evening at bedtime I had my journal and my Bible. And I wrote in that journal, two to three pages; sometimes actual quotes.

Lesson 2

THE TRUTH WILL SET YOU FREE

Summary: This lesson uses passages from 1 Corinthians 13:12 and John 8:32 to provide the foundation for you to identify what you feel to be true for yourself as a spouse caring for a husband or wife with dementia.

This lesson focuses on the uniqueness of each spouse's situation despite the common experience of being a caregiver. Please remember that how one person makes sense of their situation may look different compared to someone else in the group. As participants share how they view their marriage and cope with their caregiving challenges, you may discover that what works for you (based on your "truths") may not work for someone else. Keep an open mind. You may also discover new ways to perceive and approach your own situation.

Goals
- Identify your feelings.
- Explore the uniqueness of each person's experience of caregiving and understanding of marriage.

Materials
- Large sheets of paper
- Marker
- One large, irregularly shaped rock, or any item that looks different from various angles (a sculpture, a shoe turned on its side, etc.)

Lesson
A. Discuss:
1. When did you encounter a particularly dark time in your life? What made it so? How did it end?
2. How do you tend to cope with challenges?
B. Read aloud 1 Corinthians 13:12:
For now we see only a reflection as in a mirror; then we shall see face to face. Now I know in part; then I shall know fully, even as I am fully known.

C. Discuss:
1. What can you "not see" (make sense of) with regard to your spouse's dementia?
2. How comfortable are you not knowing what the future holds?
3. On the top of a large sheet of paper, write "I know this to be true." (For example: "I know that God loves me.") Take turns sharing what beliefs you have that you find to be true for you. Another way to think about this is: What do you have faith in? What sustains you? Write down the responses.
4. Discuss: How do these truths relate to being married to someone with dementia?

D. Read aloud John 8:32:
Then you will know the truth, and the truth will set you free.

E. Discuss:
1. How do the truths you have just identified set you free?
2. Finish the sentence: "Lord, I believe. Help thou my _____" (Mark 9:24, KJV).
3. Do you ever struggle with knowing something to be true in your head but have trouble feeling it in your heart?

4. What message from God would you most like to hear right now?

F. On the top of another large sheet of paper, write "Emotions Related to Caregiving."

G. Read over the list of emotions below.

1. Write down the emotions that stand out to you as common responses to caregiving.

2. Are there any emotions not listed that you would like to include?

3. List any additional emotions. (Keep this list for week 5.)

Accepting   Agitated   Ambivalent   Angry   Annoyed
Anxious   Appreciative   Ashamed   Bitter   Confused
Content   Courageous   Delighted   Depressed
Deserted   Despairing   Disappointed   Distrustful
Elated   Embarrassed   Emotional   Envious   Fearful
Frustrated   Generous   Grateful   Guilty   Happy
Helpless   Hopeful   Hopeless   Hostile   Hurt   Inadequate
Insecure   Insulted   Jealous   Joyful   Lonely   Longing
Loved   Misunderstood   Needy   Nervous   Peaceful
Pleased   Quarrelsome   Regretful   Rejected   Relieved
Remorseful   Repulsed   Resentful   Resigned   Sad
Satisfied   Shy   Spiritual   Tense   Tired   Wary   Worried
Worthless

Add your own:

_____

_____

_____

_____

4. Refer to this list of emotions while taking turns reading the Personal Narratives aloud. For each narrative, discuss:

5. What stands out to you in this narrative?

6. What emotions are being expressed? Can you relate? How or how not?

7. Which emotions have you listed, or that you identify with from the narratives, lack a sense of hope? How might God see your situation differently?

H. Reflection—The intimacy of marriage lends itself to very personal emotions and choices regarding how to balance providing the best care for your spouse while also taking care of yourself. In preparation for Lesson 3, you are invited to reflect upon your choices in caregiving (which are based on your unique set of circumstances), and you are encouraged to take time to consider the choices other spouses may make based on *their* unique set of circumstances. The following exercise helps with this.

1. Place a large rock, shoe, or other irregularly shaped object in the center of the group.

2. Ask members of the group to describe the item from their perspective in detail.

3. Read aloud the following:

    There is a Native American tradition where a rock is placed in the center of a group sitting in a circle. Each person then shares with the group their description of the rock. One person may see it as a large, rugged dome; another may see a flat surface; yet another may see cracks and crevices. Each person offers their different perspective of the same rock. Without listening to the different viewpoints from everyone in the group, each individual might only see the rock from their one point of view and assume it must be the same for others. The purpose of this exercise is to demonstrate that we all see situations from our own unique view. We bring to any circumstance our own history and our limitations and biases, but also our own experience and knowledge. Our interpretation of any event is not any more or less valuable than another's. And how we act based on those perspectives is uniquely our action. Just as it is for everyone else. Our viewpoints are all meaningful in their own way, and when we are willing to hear one another's perspectives without judgment, we become teachable and may discover tools to help us on our own journey.

I. Recite together in prayer: *God, I know you created me in your image and that the gift of emotion is part of being human. Help me to acknowledge what I am feeling and realize that emotions are not meant to make me feel more separated from you, but are provided by you so that I can feel my way closer to you. Lord, today I give my burdens to you and will be attentive to your guidance this week for how I can see my situation through your eyes. Amen.*

Lesson 2
Personal Narratives

After each narrative, ask yourself, "What stands out to me about this narrative?"

1.

When I got married, my father said, "Now when you marry, you go with your husband. That is your place." Nowadays, that's not exactly a women's lib quote, is it? The staff at the nursing home tell me, "You don't have to come every day." But if I miss a day, I worry about how my husband is doing, and I would feel so guilty! My girlfriends are trying to get me to take a five-day cruise with them. I can't imagine the luxury of doing something for myself.

2.

I know I need more patience, but sometimes he acts like a child, and I just want to grab him by the shoulders and shake some sense into him!

3.

Selfishly, I kind of wish God would just go ahead and take me. Seventy-four years in this world is long enough. But then who would take care of Mary? Those are the thoughts that keep me awake at night.

4.

Caring for my wife, if anything, has brought me closer to God and to my daughters. Agnes took care us for many years and did an amazing job raising the kids. It's my turn to take care of her.

5.

I am overwhelmed by it all—searching for resources (attorneys, multiple doctors, etc.), attending to all the physical, hands-on care that keeps me busy every day. When my kids were toddlers, my exhaustion lessened as they became older and more independent. But with my husband, he's only going to get more dependent on me as time goes on. Quite honestly, I am afraid for what the future may hold.

6.

My wife and I got married a few years ago. We both had lost our spouses and decided it would be nice to have companionship, so we got married. I love her, but not the same way I loved my first wife. Now she's been diagnosed with Lewy-Body dementia and, boy, can she be mean! I have arthritis in my knees, and the other week, something set her off, and she came after me with a wooden spoon. I could barely run away! I'm starting to tour dementia care units, but her kids (who live out of state) think I'm pretty rotten for considering it.

Lesson 3

WAYS TO EXPRESS COMMITMENT

Summary: The purpose of marriage has changed drastically over the years. Historically, marriage was used to strengthen an alliance between families, for economic security, or to produce an heir. Eventually, society came to see marriage as more of an institution based on love, not social constructs. This week you will consider the reasons you chose to get married and what the commitment of marriage means to you.

Goals
- Explore how Jesus understood marriage.
- Name the changes that can occur in a marriage as a result of one spouse being diagnosed with dementia.

- Discuss and apply Jesus' teachings on marriage.
- Name different types of commitments.
- Identify one's own understanding of commitment.

Materials
- Large sheets of paper
- Marker

Lesson
A. Ask:
1. Which sitcom on TV (past or present) portrays your favorite image of marriage? Why?
2. Who has demonstrated the best marriage in your life? How so?

B. Discuss the following questions:
1. How do you define marriage?
2. Has your definition changed during the course of your marriage? Since the onset of dementia?
3. Why did you get married? Have you stayed married for the same reasons?
4. What are some of the biggest changes that have occurred in your marriage since your spouse's diagnosis of Alzheimer's?

C. Read aloud Matthew 22:23–33:

> That same day the Sadducees, who say there is no resurrection, came to him with a question. "Teacher," they said, "Moses told us that if a man dies without having children, his brother must marry the widow and raise up offspring for him. Now there were seven brothers among us. The first one married and died, and since he had no children, he left his wife to his brother. The same thing happened to the second and third brother, right on down to the seventh. Finally, the woman died. Now then, at the resurrection, whose wife will she be of the seven, since all of them were married to her?" Jesus replied, "You are in error because you do not know the Scriptures or the power of God. At the resurrection people will neither marry nor be given in marriage; they will be like the angels in heaven. But about the resurrection of the dead—have you not read what God said to you, 'I am the God of Abraham, the God of Isaac, and the God of Jacob'? He is not the God of the dead but of the living." When the crowds heard this, they were astonished at his teaching.

D. Discuss:

   1. Why do you think there is no marriage in heaven?
   2. For you, what makes marriage unique compared to other relationships?

3. Does this passage impact your understanding of your marriage in any way? If so, how?

E. Personal Narratives

1. Write the title "Marital Commitments" on a large sheet of paper.

2. Take turns reading the Personal Narratives aloud. For each one, consider: "What stands out to you about this narrative?" Identify the type of commitment the caregiver has for their spouse (for example, commitment to a promise, to the person, to an ideal…). List these commitments on the sheet of paper.

3. Ask:

   a. What commitments are most important to you in your marriage?

   b. How can others help you keep those commitments?

F. Recite together in prayer: *Lord, may our commitment to you and your commandment to love one another surpass all of our relationships and guide us to make choices that best serve you and our loved ones. Amen.*

Lesson 3
Personal Narratives

After each narrative, ask yourself, "What stands out to me about this narrative?"

1.

My husband is the only person I have ever loved. I guess you could call us "soulmates." I cannot imagine someone else caring for him. It isn't easy, but it is an honor. I know he would do the same for me. My sister keeps saying, "Be careful. You know what they say, 'Caregiving kills the caregiver.'" I don't care. I love him.

2.

It's kind of like you lost her as a spouse...It's more of an obligation, a family obligation than it is a spousal relationship... It's more sympathy on my part, and feeling a strong obligation to her, but she...you know...I'll take care of her for the rest of her life...There's a responsibility, but there's no relationship.

3.

I've become a mother to my husband instead of a wife. I find it's difficult to make this role change at this point in my life. In the attempt, I feel I'm not my usual self. I seem to have other thoughts that are taking over. They are sad and depressing, and I don't like the feeling. I feel very sorry for myself because I can't be what my husband needs me to be. I don't have the commitment, as you would have, for example, for a sick child. I don't have the strength anymore. I don't have the strength anymore to be a "mother" in that way, and certainly not to my husband.

4.

I met a nice woman, Karen, whose husband is also in the dementia care unit at the nursing home. We usually arrive at the same time to feed our spouses. Neither her husband nor my wife remembers that we are their spouse. Sometimes my wife thinks I'm her brother. One time Karen's husband introduced her to his "wife" (another resident at the facility). That was pretty rough on Karen. I wish I could become better friends with her outside of the nursing home; she is the only other person who truly understands what it is like to be married to someone who doesn't know you. But I'm too worried about what other people would think.

5.

To me, sacrifice is the essence of marital love. It's not the essence, but it's part of it: doing what pleases the beloved. It's not just in sex; it's in everything. You do what pleases the beloved. If something bugs you, then I need to change. I need to, if for love's sake, change the way I do things…for you. You know we start out life—all of life is a loss, isn't it? We lose our hair, we lose our teeth, we lose our appearance, we lose our job, we lose a loved one. All of all of life is a losing process. But in Christ there is always a purpose even in the losing. Faith in Christ trumps all of that because we know that this is…we are temporary, and we are all terminal. We're going to die of something…Jesus was the consummate [sufferer]. All the people in the Scriptures who were usable by God were sufferers. He allowed them to be put through the hoops; including his own son. He suffered more than any of us. If Jesus suffered, I can glorify him by suffering, too.

Lesson 4

FINDING PEACE

Summary: This last lesson offers hope as you continue your caregiving journey. Jeremiah's theme of ambassadorship is introduced to offer support in your role as spousal caregivers. The group will be asked to list ways others can help you so that you have more peace in your lives. In week 5 you will be asked to share this list with your church. By presenting a list that comes out of the whole group, no one person is singled out, and the church has a clearer understanding of how they can minister more directly and efficiently to dementia caregivers.

Goals

- Define *peace*.
- Identify specific ways your church can help you experience a greater sense of peace.
- Affirm God's commitment to us.
- Consider our role as God's ambassadors.

Materials

- Bibles
- Large sheets of paper
- Marker
- Notebook-sized paper for each participant
- Pens

Lesson

A. Read aloud John 14:27:

Peace I leave with you; my peace I give you. I do not give to you as the world gives. Do not let your hearts be troubled and do not be afraid.

B. Discuss:

1. What does *peace* mean for you?
2. On a scale of 1 to 10, with 1 representing no peace and 10 being completely at peace, where would you rate yourself?
3. In what ways would you like to have more peace?

C. Jeremiah 29:4–7

   1. Read aloud the various translations of Jeremiah 29:4–7 and then the excerpt from Dr. Robert Linthicum's talk "Seeking Shalom in the City to Which You Have Been Called" on the following pages.

   2. Discuss:

      a. How is your experience as a caregiver similar to the experience of the Israelites?

      b. Linthicum focuses on the word Hebrew word *galah* (*gaw'law*), which can mean "sent" or "exiled." Which way do you feel regarding your situation as a caregiver?

      c. How does your perception of your role as a caregiver change when you consider yourself *sent* to your situation verses *exiled* to it?

      d. How can you seek the peace and prosperity in the place to which you have been called? How can your church help?

      e. One a large sheet of paper, write the title "How Others Can Help." Don't be afraid to list both general needs as well as seemingly simple, mundane ones. Members of the Providing Sanctuary group have compiled a list of gifts they have to share, and the more items on your list, the higher the likelihood someone has a gift that perfectly matches your need! Additionally, it is often true that others want to help, but they need to know *how*. That is where your list will be extremely helpful. Bring this list to the week 5 gathering.

D. Pass out a sheet of paper and pen to each participant. Take some time to go back and review the Personal Narratives from the first three lessons.

1. Which narrative(s) stood out to you? Why do you think this is?

2. Picture the most hopeful scenario you would like to see for you and your spouse 6 months from now. On your paper, describe what that scenario would look like. You are encouraged to keep this paper and review it from time to time.

3. If you feel comfortable, share your scenario with the group.

E. Closing

1. Celebrate the group's four weeks together. Invite participants to share responses or feedback.

2. Recite together in prayer: *Lord, thank you for the fellowship of these past four weeks. May we go forth from this place with a greater sense of hope. Thank you for bringing us this far. May we always remember*

that others journey alongside us, and may we have the courage to reach out to others when we need you the most. Amen.

Jeremiah 29:4–7

New International Version

This is what the Lord Almighty, the God of Israel, says to all those I carried into exile from Jerusalem to Babylon: "Build houses and settle down; plant gardens and eat what they produce. Marry and have sons and daughters; find wives for your sons and give your daughters in marriage, so that they too may have sons and daughters. Increase in number there; do not decrease. Also, seek the peace and prosperity of the city to which I have carried you into exile. Pray to the Lord for it, because if it prospers, you too will prosper."

King James Version

Thus, saith the Lord of hosts, the God of Israel, unto all that are carried away captives, whom I have caused to be carried away from Jerusalem unto Babylon; Build ye houses, and dwell in them; and plant gardens, and eat the fruit of them; Take ye wives, and beget sons and daughters; and take wives for your sons, and give your daughters to husbands, that they may bear sons and daughters; that ye may be increased there, and not diminished. And seek the peace of the city whither I have caused you to be carried away captives, and pray unto the Lord for it: for in the peace thereof shall ye have peace.

New English Translation

The Lord of Heaven's Armies, the God of Israel, says to all those he sent into exile to Babylon from Jerusalem, "Build houses and settle down. Plant gardens and eat what they produce. Marry and have sons and daughters. Find wives for your sons and allow your daughters to get married so that they too can have sons and daughters. Grow in number; do not dwindle away. Work to see that the city where I sent you as exiles enjoys peace and prosperity. Pray to the Lord for it. For as it prospers you will prosper."

Excerpt from
"Seeking Shalom in the City to
Which You Have Been Called"
by Dr. Robert Linthicum

These folks want to go back home again. And what is God through Jeremiah telling them?..."You aren't going back home for another 70 years...[In other words] You're not going back home...you're going to die here."...And then God has the temerity to say, "But I have good news for you!"...So the question is, "Where's the good news?"...Well, it's found in verse 7...What does your text say? "Carry," "sent," "ordered," "deported"...Anybody have "sent into exile"? All right, I mean, what's the matter with these translators? Can't they make up their mind? "Sent," "called," "deported," "sent into exile." Don't these translators know a good Jewish word when they see it? Well, the fact is, they do, and that's why they're having such a big problem. That's why they're coming up with all these different translations. Because there is no English equivalent of the Hebrew word that occurs at this point. And so, the only way they can translate it is to approximate it with a bunch of English words that get around the topic, but none of them hit it squarely because we don't have any word for what's in there. It's pretty important that we know what it is because it's telling us why we're in the city as God's people...The Hebrew word actually has two nuances to it…It means "exiled" but it also means "sent," and *it is used for an ambassador*…God uses our circumstances in order to enable us to carry out the call God has given us…You, as a Christian, are in the city in which you live because God has called you there as his ambassador, and that's what Jeremiah chapter 29 verse 7 is saying. Seek the shalom of the city where I have sent you using the circumstance of exile.[6]

---

6   Robert Linthicum, "Seeking Shalom in the City to Which You Have Been Called," Doctor of Ministry Intensive, Faith in Action in the City, United Theological Seminary, Dayton, Ohio, Plenary Session I, Tuesday, January 25, 2005.

PART IV

CREATING SANCTUARY

DESIGNING A DEMENTIA
CAREGIVER MINISTRY

Summary: Creating Sanctuary is a coming together of the Providing Sanctuary and Seeking Sanctuary groups. This combined session (ideally preceded by a potluck meal!) provides the opportunity for congregants to share with the family caregivers what they learned from walking in their shoes through the Personal Narratives. Caregivers are invited to provide additional information and feedback and share how their congregations can best support them. Each group should assign a delegate from their group to guide the discussion, although everyone is encouraged to participate and provide feedback.

Goals

- Create the framework for an amazing ministry for dementia caregivers.
- Identify members willing to provide leadership.

Materials

- Lists compiled from the previous weeks from each group
- Large sheets of paper
- Several markers

Meeting

A. Post all the lists created from previous weeks at the front of the room. Assess the experience of each of the groups, using the lists to invite discussion. Ask such questions as:

1. What were some things you learned during the last four weeks that you did not know before?

2. Where are some of the most pressing challenges and needs within our congregation?

3. Were there any challenges or needs identified within your group that surprised you?

4. What are some of the spiritual gifts identified by the Providing Sanctuary group?

B. Separate into groups of three or four, making sure
    that each group has members from both the Providing
    and Seeking groups. Give each group a large sheet
    of paper, and at the top write "Ideas for Ministry."
    Based on the information provided on the lists and
    today's discussion, give each group 10–15 minutes to
    list ideas for ministries based on the needs and gifts
    listed. After 10 minutes, have groups swap their sheet
    with another group and allow another 10 minutes for
    groups to add ideas.

    Here are just a few ideas that have come out of creative
    congregations:

    •   Build activity boards or "busy boxes" filled with
        manipulatives such as locks, switches, magnets,
        and so on to keep loved ones occupied.

    •   Create a card ministry to send encouraging notes
        to caregivers.

    •   Offer to sit with a person with dementia for an
        hour or two so their caregiver can take a walk, run
        errands, or care for themselves in some way.

    •   Have caregivers and their loved ones gather at
        the church to compile church bulletins or do
        another simple task each week. (This provides
        the opportunity for people with dementia to feel

like they are doing something useful while their caregivers have the chance to mingle with others experiencing a similar situation.)

- Bring communion to those unable to attend church.

C. After completing the lists of ministry ideas, identify two to five items that address the most prevalent needs that have been identified in your congregation. List each of these ministry ideas on their own sheet of paper, and prepare an additional paper that says "Other" at the top.

D. Enter into a time of reflection and prayer. While participants sit quietly with their eyes closed, have the pastor or another leader pray, *Lord, we have gathered here because either we are in need or we have a gift to share—perhaps both. It is not easy to ask for help, but you commission us to serve others, and we know that in serving others, we serve you. Wonderfully, we know that in serving you through the gifts you have given to each one of us, we can find a joy like no other. Thank you for the vulnerability others have shown us. Thank you for the fellowship we have found these past several weeks. Mostly, thank you for the miracle of love you are about to reveal as we commit to participating in acts that will bring strength and hope to another. In blessing others, may we truly be blessed. Amen.*

E. Invite those present to come forward and write their names on one of the ministry sheets, indicating their interest in serving on that ministry. For those interested in serving in another way, have them to write their name on the Other sheet and indicate next to their name how they would like to help.

F. Identify two people on each sheet who are willing to organize their group and meet in the coming weeks to come up with a plan of action.

This week is purposely not very structured because this is where Finding Sanctuary in the Midst of Alzheimer's becomes individualized for your church. Every congregation is made up of unique individuals with unique gifts. The goal this week is to explore where the challenges, needs, and gifts intersect. Prayer, brainstorming, and out-of-the-box thinking should guide your discussion. Please share your ministry ideas and stories at www. sanctuaryinthemidst.com.

May God bless you in this ministry!

A FINAL WORD

There are two common concerns I encounter while working with both caregivers and with those who have a friend diagnosed with dementia.

The first is repetitiveness and general confusion. It can drive a family member crazy when their loved one asks over and over, "What day is it?" or "When is lunch?" Sometimes the role you play as a caregiver entails some imagining when it comes to relating to a person with dementia. I say *imagining* (an action verb) instead of *imagination* (a noun) because it is your response—your action—that will often determine the course of a conversation that makes no sense to you. Remember, providing care for someone with dementia is not about being logical; it's about providing assurance. So, when your wife asks you 10 times if you are going to the grocery store, imagine each time she asks like it's the very first time she's asking (because for her it is!), Then answer her *every time* as if it is the first time you are answering her. Is it repetitive to answer the same way over and over? Yes. But if you answer her and then say, "You just asked me that!" then you are choosing to add the element of frustration, and that doesn't help either of you. I know it's not easy. But I encourage you to practice this—it truly will help. And chances are, you will have lots of opportunities to practice!

Or, when your father insists that his father (who died 20 years ago) is coming in his car to pick him up, don't argue to change what doesn't make sense to *you*; instead *imagine* the meaning your deceased grandfather is having for your dad at that moment. Rather than dashing his plans and telling him that his father couldn't possibly be picking him up because he is no longer living, explore where your dad is currently dwelling in his mind; perhaps ask him what he enjoyed about car rides with his father when he was younger. Ask him if he remembers his first car, places his father would take him, and so on. When you respond to confused loved ones with the intention of providing assurance rather than setting them straight, you will both enjoy your interactions more.

The second thing I encounter is the falling away of friends when someone is diagnosed with dementia. So often, people in uncomfortable situations don't know what to say, so they don't say anything. A central purpose of *Finding Sanctuary in the Midst of Alzheimer's* is to equip others to be more supportive of caregivers, and one of the best ways to do this is to tackle your own insecurities. It can be uncomfortable interacting with someone you may have played bridge with for years but who now does not remember how to hold a fork properly, let alone a hand of cards. I have found it helpful to dispose of any notion that you need to know how to engage with a person with dementia in order to make the interaction meaningful. One of the best words of advice I ever received was during my training to be a healthcare chaplain. At that time, it was very scary for me to think about encountering patients in the hospital who were experiencing life-threatening situations. I worried about not being helpful to them or, worse, saying something that would cause emotional or spiritual harm. My supervisor, Sheryl, gave these instructions: "Before you enter a patient's room ask yourself, 'What is this person going to teach me about myself?'" Approaching someone with the intention of learning about yourself does two things: First, it takes the pressure off of you for feeling like you need to act a certain way, and second, it makes you teachable. So often, going toward what makes us uncomfortable provides us with the most amazing experiences. In your effort to engage with someone who might make you feel uncomfortable, may you know that just showing up is often the best thing you can offer—and then be open to what God may have to teach you.

ABOUT THE AUTHOR

Dr. Elizabeth Shulman has 30 years of experience in both parish and healthcare ministry. Her devotions for caregivers have appeared in Guideposts' *Strength and Grace*, and she frequently speaks to churches, retirement communities, and other community groups on dementia and caregiving. A spousal caregiver for eight years, she now trains congregations to be more comfortable and confident in ministering to families impacted by dementia. Her presentations *Mary and Martha Caregiving* and *A New Pair of Glasses* inform audience members on the challenges of caregiving and offer hope to caregivers by providing new ways to reframe their experience. She and her husband, Leo, share seven wonderful daughters and live near Cleveland, Ohio. To find out more, please visit her website: www.elizabethshulman.com.

A free ebook edition is available with the purchase of this book.

To claim your free ebook edition:

1. Visit MorganJamesBOGO.com
2. Sign your name CLEARLY in the space
3. Complete the form and submit a photo of the entire copyright page
4. You or your friend can download the ebook to your preferred device

A **FREE** ebook edition is available for you or a friend with the purchase of this print book.

CLEARLY SIGN YOUR NAME ABOVE

Instructions to claim your free ebook edition:
1. Visit MorganJamesBOGO.com
2. Sign your name CLEARLY in the space above
3. Complete the form and submit a photo of this entire page
4. You or your friend can download the ebook to your preferred device

Print & Digital Together Forever.

Snap a photo

Free ebook

Read anywhere

CPSIA information can be obtained
at www.ICGtesting.com
Printed in the USA
JSHW021917151121
20473JS00004B/179

9 781631 954634